How to Implement Management by Objectives in Your Business

A Step by Step Guide to Implementing MBO

By Meir Liraz

(Including 10 Special Bonuses)

Published by Liraz Publishing

www.BizMove.com

Copyright © Liraz Publishing. All rights reserved.

ISBN: 9781695654525

Table of Contents

1. Introduction — 5
2. What Business Am I In? — 8
3. The Complete MBO Program — 10
4. Goal Setting — 12
5. The Miniature Work Plan — 14
6. Kinds of Goals — 17
7. Progress Reports — 20
8. Performance Evaluation — 22
9. Installing MBO — 23
10. Threats to the MBO System — 25

Supplements:

11. How to Make the Right Decisions — 26
12. Improving Your Delegation Skills — 32

Appendix: Special Free Bonuses — 37

MEIR LIRAZ

1. Introduction

Many authorities on business management identify five functions of management:

planning,

organizing,

directing,

controlling, and

coordinating.

The planning and controlling functions often get less attention from owner-managers of businesses than they should. One way to strengthen both of these functions is through effective goal setting.

Long range goals for sales, profits, competitive position, development of people, and industrial relations must be established. Then, goals are set for the current year which will lead towards the accomplishment of the long range goals.

This Guide presents Management by Objectives to the owner-manager of a company for use in this type of planning and goal setting. MBO includes goal setting by all managers down to the first level of supervision. Their goals are tied to those of the company.

Traditionally, people have worked according to job descriptions that list the activities of the job. The Management by Objectives (MBO) approach, on the other hand, stresses results.

Let's look at an example. Suppose that you have a credit manager and that his or her job description simply says that the credit manager supervises the credit operations of the company. The activities of the credit manager are then listed. Under MBO, the credit manager could have five or six goals covering important aspects of the work. One goal might be to increase credit sales enough to support a 15 percent increase in sales.

The traditional job description for a personnel specialist might include language about conducting the recruiting program for your company. Under MBO, the specialist's work might be covered in five or six goals - one which could be "recruit five new employees in specified categories by July 1."

Thus, MBO looks for results, not activities. With MBO, you view the job in terms of what it should achieve. Activity is never the essential element. It is merely an intermediate step leading to the desired result.

2. What Business Am I In?

In making long range plans, the first question you ought to think about is "what business am I in?" Is the definition you have of your business is right for today's market?

Are there emerging customer needs that will require a changed definition of your business next year?

For example, one owner-manager's business was making metal trash cans. When sales began to fall off, the owner was forced to reexamine the business. To regain lost sales and continue to grow the owner redefined the product as metal containers and developed a marketing plan for that product.

How you view your business will provide the framework for your planning with respect to markets, product development, buildings and equipment, financial needs, and staff size.

Your long range objectives for your business will be the cornerstone in the MBO program for your company. At a minimum, they must be clearly communicated to your managers; however, for a truly vital program your managers should have a part in formulating these long range goals. Your managers will base their short range goals on these objectives. If they have had a role in establishing the long range objectives, they will be more committed to achieving them.

3. The Complete MBO Program

Management by Objectives may be used in all kinds of organizations. But not everyone has had the same degree of success in using this concept. From examining those MBO programs that failed, it is clear that the programs were incomplete.

The minimum requirements for an MBO program are:

Each manager's job includes five to ten goals expressed in specific, measurable terms.

Each manager reporting to you proposes his or her goals to you in writing. When you both agree on each goal, a final written statement of the goal is prepared.

Each goal consists of the statement of the goal, how it will be measured, and the work steps necessary to complete it.

Results are systematically determine at regular intervals (at least quarterly) and compared with the goals.

When progress towards goals is not in accordance with your plans, problems are identified and corrective action is taken.

Goals at each level of management are related to the level above and the level below.

4. Goal Setting

Goals for each of your managers are the crucial element in any MBO system. Goals at middle level of management must be consistent with those at top levels. Goals of first line supervisors must relate to those at middle levels. Goals prepared by the manager responsible for certain steps in a large processing operation must tie in with those of managers responsible for other steps in the processing. And all goals must relate to and support your long range objectives for the company.

When all these goals are consistent, then an MBO system will be developed. Until then, there will be many like the middle manager of a research and development company who exclaimed in a seminar, "How can I set my goals when I don't know where top management wants to go?"

Each manager will probably find between five and eight goals enough to cover those aspects of the job crucial to successful performance. These are the elements which you will use to judge his or her performance. Of course, other duties which do not fall into the above goals should not be neglected. But they are of secondary importance.

When you first start your MBO program, your managers will undergo a learning period. They must learn how to prepare a goal which will make them stretch but is not beyond their capabilities. They must learn to develop ways to effectively measure real problems which threaten the achievement of the goals and then take steps to cope with the problems.

During this learning period, your managers should first set a few goals. Then as they learn how to develop and achieve goals, the coverage and number of goals can be extended.

5. The Miniature Work Plan

Your managers may find the miniature work plan useful. On this work plan the manager can show each of the major work steps (sub-goals) necessary to reach the goal. Then, if each work step is performed by the indicated date, the goal will be reached when the last work step is completed.

You may also use this form to discuss goals with your manager. By looking at this form, you can see not only the goal but also the plan for reaching that goal. This will allow you to ask questions about the work steps and anticipated problems, as well as to question how the goal will be measured. By pointing out the relationship between the manager's goal and your goal, you'll be helping each of your managers to understand how his/her goals relate to those of the company.

A Manager's Goal

Instructions for Completing Form

Management by Objectives provides for the establishment of four to ten goals by each manager. You should set up goals in each of several important areas in your job. You might try to establish at least one in each of these categories: Regular, Problem Solving, Innovative, and Development. By following this approach you will be more likely to see the full range of possibilities open to you through goal setting.

Develop each goal as a miniature work plan. The steps that follow will result in goals which are complete and useful to both you and your boss.

Goal (Be specific and concise)

_____

_____

Measurement (The bench mark that tells you that you have achieved the goal, should be expressed in quantitative terms)

_____

_____

Major Problems Anticipated

_____

_____

_____

Work Steps (List three or four most essential steps, give completion dates for each)

_____

_____

_____

_____

Superior's Goal (Give goal at next higher level to which your goal relates).

_____

_____

_____

Whenever a problem is listed on the work plan, the manager should include a work step to deal with it. For example, suppose the head of your supply department set a goal to deliver all packages within one day of when they were received. He thought he might have difficulty in getting his people to follow the new procedures. So, he included a work step to teach these procedures before the new program went into effect.

6. Kinds of Goals

When your managers begin to set their goals, they may want to know what areas are suitable for goal setting. What are the really important aspects of their jobs rather than that part which is most visible to them? How can they be sure that their program is balanced for the long haul, rather than just reacting to immediate, pressing problems? How can they set goals which are most likely to help them control their jobs?

It might be useful for them to have a classification of goals that suggests areas of opportunity. Generally, each manager should have between five and eight goals. One or two goals in each of these areas should be helpful:

1. Regular work goals.

2. Problem solving goals.

3. Innovative goals.

4. Development goals.

Regular work refers to those activities which make up the major part of the manager's responsibilities. The head of production would be primarily concerned with the amount, quality, and efficiency of production. The head of marketing would be primarily concerned with developing and conducting the market research and sales programs. Each manager should be able to find opportunities to operate more efficiently, to improve the quality of the product or service, and to expand the total amount produced or marketed.

Problem solving goals will give your managers an opportunity to define their major problems. There is no danger of anyone ever running out of problems. New problems or new versions of old problems always seem to replace those overcome.

Innovative goals may be viewed the same way. A goal for innovation may apply to an actual problem. But, some innovation may not deal with a problem. For example, the head of building management sets a goal to invigorate the employee suggestion program by putting five suggestions into effect during the next four months. There was no specific to be solved, the manager was just trying to do the best job possible.

The development goal recognizes how important the development of your employees is to your business. Your managers can be encouraged to develop their people just as they are to produce more effectively. Every manager must be to some extent a teacher and a coach; each manager must plan for the employees' continued growth in both technical area and in working together effectively.

By asking your managers to set at least one goal in the four areas listed above, you may open their eyes to possibilities they had not seen before. the goal setting process can be a very useful educational step, even for those who are primarily specialists.

7. Progress Reports

An MBO program without provision for regular reports on progress is worthless. That is why some articles and books on MBO call the concept MBO/R. The "R" refers to results. Nothing is accomplished by setting goals or objectives unless the program calls for a regular review of progress towards results.

A large organization issued nearly 100 pages of goals prepared by many of its managers. Most of the goals were well developed. The document was very impressive. But there was absolutely no provision for a reporting system of any kind. It is easy to imagine the reaction of those who set goals for the first year when they were asked the following year to draw up new goals.

A monthly or quarterly review of progress towards goals will help you determine where progress is below expectations. For example, suppose that one of your goals calls for a reduction of overtime by 50 percent this year, and the first quarter reduction is only 15 percent. A special effort must be exerted in the succeeding quarters to regain the lost ground or the goal will not be achieved by the end of the year.

When progress is below expectations, the problem or problems holding back progress should be identified and assigned to someone, usually the manager, for resolution. Make these assignments part of the company MBO files so that responsibility for correcting the problem areas cannot be evaded.

8. Performance Evaluation

You will have to evaluate the performance of every person working for you in some way, either formally or informally. When your managers are working to achieve a full set of five to eight goals, their ability to get results on each goal can be a good, objective measure of performance.

Traditional performance evaluation systems have been strongly criticized because they deal with subjective matters such as leadership qualities, rather than the more objective measure of results. Evaluating performance by MBO, while objective, is a complex task, which must be undertaken with care by someone who fully understands MBO. Failure to reach goals can be a result of setting the wrong objectives in the first place, the existence of organizational restrictions not taken into account, inadequate or improper measures of goal achievement, personal failure, or a combination of factors.

9. Installing MBO

When installing an MBO program, many owner-managers have found it best to start their jobs by asking their managers to define their jobs. What are their major responsibilities? Then, for each responsibility, the manager and the boss decide how they will measure performance in terms of results.

The result of this exercise may surprise you. Often managers and their bosses do not even agree on the manager's major responsibilities. Also, you may find that no one is performing some of the functions that you consider important.

As the owner-manager, you must appreciate what the system will do. You have to show interest in the concept from the beginning. You have to set the example for your subordinate managers, if the MBO system is to be a success

The education of your managers may be a formidable task. They have probably thought in terms of specific functions - managing a sales department, directing a credit office - rather than in terms of goals which contribute to the organization.

It might be best to start with a seminar of six to

nine hours in a classroom. This ought to be enough to introduce MBO to the managers who will be setting goals. Either you or a consultant might conduct the seminar. (If you choose a consultant, be sure that you are there for the entire seminar).

Provide enough time so that your managers can express their doubts, reservations or opposition to MBO. It is best to get their feelings out into the open as soon as possible. Other participants can help them deal with their concerns.

A very useful part of such a seminar is the preparation of an actual goal by each participant. In small group sessions, your mangers can help each other by reviewing work plans and offering suggestions to improve each others plans.

Working with goal setting, periodic review of goals, and other aspects of MBO will be a learning experience for most managers. If they set annual goals, it may take three to four years before good results from this system of managing appear. MBO may look simple on the surface, but it requires experience and skill to make it work effectively.

10. Threats to the MBO System

Not all MBO programs are successful. Some of the leading reasons why past programs failed to reach their potential are:

1. Top management did not get involved.

2. Corporate objectives were inadequate.

3. MBO was installed as a crash program.

4. It was difficult to learn the system because the nature of MBO was not taught.

It is hard to get people to think in terms of results rather than activities relating to their work. However, it can be done. The sequence of steps one owner-manager uses may not work for another. It is often an individual matter. Results are what count.

If you feel that you are ready to introduce MBO to your company, why not set this as a goal for yourself. Turn back and follow through the work plan. List your goal, measurement, anticipated problems, and the work steps necessary to get your company managing by objectives.

11. How to Make the Right Decisions

Everyone is a decision maker. We all rely on information, and techniques or tools, to help us in our daily lives. When we go out to eat, the restaurant menu is the tool that provides us with the information needed to decide what to purchase and how much to spend. Operating a business also requires making decisions using information and techniques - how much inventory to maintain, what price to sell it at, what credit arrangements to offer, how many people to hire.

Decision making in business is the systematic process of identifying and solving problems, of asking questions and finding answers. Decisions usually are made under conditions of uncertainty. The future is not known and sometimes even the past is suspect. This guide opens the door for business owners and managers to learn about the variety of techniques which can be used to improve decision making in a world of uncertainty, change, and uncontrollable circumstances.

A General Approach to Decision Making

Whether a scientist, an executive of a major corporation, or a small business owner, the general approach to systematically solving problems is the same. The following 7 step approach to better management decision making can be used to study nearly all problems faced by a business.

1. State the problem

A problem first must exist and be recognized. What is the problem and why is it a problem. What is ideal and how do current operations vary from that ideal. Identify why the symptoms (what is going wrong) and the causes (why is it going wrong). Try to define all terms, concepts, variables, and relationships. Quantify the problem to the extent possible. If the problem, not accurately and quickly filling customer orders, try to determine how many orders were incorrectly filled and how long it took to fill them.

2. Define the Objectives

What are the objectives of the study. Which objectives are the most critical. Objectives usually are stated by an action verb like to reduce, to increase, or to improve. Returning to the customer order problem, the major objectives would be: 1) to increase the percentage of orders filled correctly, and 2) to reduce the time it takes to process and order. A subobjective could include to simplify and streamline the order filling process.

3. Develop a Diagnostic Framework

Next establish a diagnostic framework, that is, decide what methods are going to be used, what kinds of information are needed, and how and where the information is to be found. Is there going to be a customer survey, a review of company documents, time and motion tests, or something else. What are the assumptions (facts assumed to be correct) of the study. What are the criteria used to judge the study. What time, budget, or other constraints are there. What kind of quantitative or other specific techniques are going to be used to analyze the data. (Some of which will be covered shortly). In other words, the diagnostic framework establishes the scope and methods of the entire study.

4. Collect and Analyze the Data

The next step is to collect the data (by following the

methods established in Step 3. Raw data is then tabulated and organized to facilitate analysis. Tables, charts, graphs, indexes and matrices are some of the standard ways to organize raw data. Analysis is the critical prerequisite of sound business decision making. What does the data reveal. What facts, patterns, and trends can be seen in the data. Many of the quantitative techniques covered below can be used during the step to determine facts, patterns, and trends in data. Of course, computers are used extensively during this step.

5. Generate Alternative Solutions

After the analysis has been finished, some specific conclusions about the nature of the problem and its resolution should have been reached. The next step is to develop alternative solutions to the problem and rank them in order of their net benefits. But how are alternatives best generated. Again, there are several well established techniques such as the Nominal Group Method, the Delphi Method and Brainstorming, among others. In all these methods a group is involved, all of whom have reviewed the data and analysis. The approach is to have an informed group suggesting a variety of possible solutions.

6. Develop an Action Plan and Implement

Select the best solution to the problem but be certain to understand clearly why it is best, that is, how it achieves the objectives established in Step 2 better than its alternatives. Then develop an effective method (Action Plan) to implement the solution. At this point an important organizational consideration arises - who is going to be responsible for seeing the implementation through and what authority does he have. The selected manager should be responsible for seeing that all tasks, deadlines, and reports are performed, met, and written. Details are important in this step: schedules, reports, tasks, and communication are the key elements of any action plan. There are several techniques available to decision makers implementing an action plan. The PERT method is a way of laying out an entire period such as an action plan. PERT will be covered shortly.

7. Evaluate, obtain Feedback and Monitor

After the Action Plan has been implemented to solve a problem, management must evaluate its effectiveness. Evaluation standards must be determined, feedback channels developed, and monitoring performed. This Step should be done after 3 to 5 weeks and again at 6 months. The goal is to answer the bottom line question. Has the problem been solved?

12. Improving Your Delegation Skills

Derived from Latin, delegate means "to send from." When delegating you are sending the work "from" you "to" someone else. Effective delegation Skills will not only give you more time to work on your important opportunities, but you will also help others on your team learn new skills.

Here are some tips that will help you improve your delegation skills - delegation of work.

- Delegation helps people grow underneath you in an organization and thus pushes you even higher in management. It provides you with more time, and you will be able to take on higher priority projects.

- Delegate whole pieces or entire job pieces rather than simply tasks and activities.

- Clearly define what outcome is needed, then let individuals use some creative thinking of their own as to how to get to that outcome.

- Clearly define limits of authority that go with the delegated job. Can the person hire other people to work with them? Are there spending constraints?

- Clear standards of performance will help the person know when he or she is doing exactly what is expected.

- When on the receiving end of delegation, work to make your boss' job easier and to get the boss promoted. This will enhance your promotability also.

- Assess routine activities in which you are involved. Can any of them be eliminated or delegated?

- Never underestimate a person's potential. Delegate slightly more than you think the person is capable of handling. Expect them to succeed, and you will be pleasantly surprised more frequently than not.

- Expect completed staff work from the individuals reporting to you. That is, they will come to you giving you alternatives and suggestions when a problem exists rather than just saying "Boss, what should we do?"

- Do not avoid delegating something because you cannot give someone the entire project. Let the person start with a bite size piece, then after learning and doing that, they can accept larger pieces and larger areas of responsibility.

- Agree on a monitoring or measurement procedure that will keep you informed as to progress on this project because you are ultimately still responsible for it and need to know that it is progressing as it should. In other words-If you can't measure it don't delegate it.

- Keep your mind open to new ideas and ways of doing things. There just might be a better way than the way something has previously been done.

- Delegation is not giving an assignment. You are asking the person to accept responsibility for a project. They have the right to say no.

- Encourage your people to ask for parts of your job.

- Never take back a delegated item because you can do it better or faster. Help the other person learn to do it better.

- Agree on the frequency of feedback meetings or reports between yourself and the person to whom you are delegating. Good communication will assure ongoing success.

- Delegation strengthens your position. It shows you are doing your job as a manager-getting results with others. This makes you more promotable.

- Delegation is taking a risk that the other person might make a mistake, but people learn from mistakes and will be able to do it right the next time. Think back to a time a project was delegated to you and you messed it up. You also learned a valuable lesson.

- Find out what the talents and interests of your people are and you will be able to delegate more intelligently and effectively.

- A person will be more excited about doing a project when they came up with the idea of how to do it, than if the boss tells them how to do it.

- Be sensitive to upward delegation by your staff. When they ask you for a decision on their project, ask them to think about some alternatives which you will then discuss with them. This way responsibility for action stays with the staff member.

- Don't do an activity that someone else would be willing to do for you if you would just ask them.

- "Push" responsibility down in a caring helpful way.

- Remember, you are not the only one that can accomplish an end result. Trust others to be capable of achieving it.

- Break large jobs into manageable pieces and delegate pieces to those who can do them more readily.

- Keep following up and following through until the entire project is done. Break large jobs into manageable pieces and delegate pieces to those who can do them more readily.

- Resist the urge to solve someone else's problem. They need to learn for themselves. Give them suggestions and perhaps limits but let them take their own action.

Appendix: Special Free Bonuses

You can access your free bonuses here:

https://www.bizmove.com/bizgifts.htm

Here's what you get:

#1 How to Be a Good Manager and Leader; 120 Tips to improve your Leadership Skills (Leadership Video Guide).

Learn how to improve your leadership skills and become a better manager and leader. Here's how to be the boss people want to give 200 percent for. In this video you'll discover 120 powerful tips and strategies to motivate and inspire your people to bring out the best in them.

#2 Small Business Management: Essential Ingredients for Success (eBook Guide)

Discover scores of business management tricks, secrets and shortcuts. This Ebook guide does far more than impart knowledge - it inspires action.

#3 How to Manage Yourself for Success; 90 Tips to Better Manage Yourself and Your Time (Self Management Video Guide)

You are responsible for everything that happens in your life. Learn to accept total responsibility for yourself. If you don't manage yourself, then you are letting others have control of your life. In this video you'll discover 90 powerful tips and strategies to better manage yourself for success.

#4 80 Best Inspirational Quotes for Success (Motivational Video Guide)

For this video we scanned thousands of motivational and inspirational quotes to bring you this collection of the best 80 motivational quotes for success in life.

#5 Top 10 Habits to Adopt From Highly Successful People (Self Growth Video Guide)

In this video you'll discover the top 10 habits of highly successful people that you can adopt and achieve success in your life.

#6 Personal Branding: How to Make a Killer First Impression (Self Promotion Video Guide)

This video deals with personal branding. While promoting your personal brand, you'll discover in this video the ten most effective things you can do to make the best first impression possible.

#7 How to Advance Your Career 10 Times Faster (Career Advancement Video Guide)

The most important thing to remember about your

career today is that you need to be responsible for your own future. In this video you'll discover 10 powerful strategies to advance your career faster.

#8 How to Get Success in Life; 10 Strategies to Attract the Life You Want (Self Actualization Video Guide)

To have more, we must be more of who we are. The secret is in the doing; none of it matters until we do something about it. In this video you'll discover 10 powerful strategies to attract the life you want.

#9 A Comprehensive Package of Business Tools

Here's a collection featuring dozens of business related templates, worksheets, forms, and plans; covering finance, starting a business, marketing, business planning, sales, and general management.

#10 People Management Skills: How to Deal with Difficult Employees (Managing People Video Guide)

Problem behavior on the part of employees can erupt for a variety of reasons. In this video you'll discover the top ten ideas for dealing with difficult employees.

MEIR LIRAZ

* * * *

www.ingramcontent.com/pod-product-compliance
Lightning Source LLC
Chambersburg PA
CBHW070843220526
45466CB00002B/869